Edward
Hopper

By Karal Ann Marling

RIZZOLI ART SERIES
Series Editor: Norma Broude

Edward Hopper

(1882–1967)

The Hideous Beauty of American Places

EDWARD HOPPER was not a garrulous man under the best of circumstances. But when eager journalists seeking words of wisdom from a famous American painter climbed the four steep flights of stairs to his studio on New York's Washington Square North in the 1950s and the early 1960s, they got silence for their trouble. Or worse yet, pithy aphorisms that failed to explain the sense of terrible, empty loneliness at the heart of the America Hopper painted—a place composed of diners lurid under green fluorescent tubes, after-hours offices aglow with sinister intent, gas pumps lined up in silent witness along the sides of empty roads, seedy motel rooms, old houses left to molder away on the wrong side of the tracks, storefronts ravaged by the light of dawn. Hopperland. What did it all mean? What was it

1. *American Landscape.* 1920.
Etching. Sheet: 13 13/16 × 18 1/4". Collection of The Whitney Museum of American Art, New York. Josephine N. Hopper Bequest.

meant to mean? And what did it have to do with the life and times of the tall, stooped, silent figure who lived seventy-four steps above the pavement of Washington Square in a studio so austere, so devoid of clues, that it contained only three items: a mirror, a big homemade easel (empty when visitors came, of course), and an abandoned etching press with an old felt hat of Edward Hopper's dangling forlornly from one of the spokes? Were the pictures so still and sad because *he* was, too? Because his art was autobiography?

By the time he died in his upstairs studio in 1967, Edward Hopper had become a national treasure. In the 1960s vast numbers of ordinary Americans knew his work of the 1920s, 1930s, and 1940s through color reproductions in books and magazines. The artist's tottering mansions and failing roadside enterprises gave shape to an urgent nostalgia for a simpler era. His painted world seemed basically unchanged since the Depression and World War II: however bleak and bare, that America looked comforting to

a generation sickened by its own material wealth and its lethal technology. They were reassured, too, by Hopper's attitude toward his subject matter. Contemporary realists—the Pop artists—dared the viewer to *like* a can of soup. But that knowing, mocking edge was harder to locate in Edward Hopper. The art writers and the curators of the 1960s believed Hopper to be an astute critic of his self-selected slice of American life. Yet, like everybody else, the art establishment prized his vision, however ambiguous, however out of step with the prevailing fashion for abstraction laced with bitter quotations from commercial culture. From 1950 through his final years, a period that coincided precisely with the eclipse of the style he practiced, Hopper found himself heaped with honors. Museums held Hopper retrospective exhibitions. When he protested the preponderance of abstract "gobbledegook" on the walls of New York City's major museums, he alone was given a respectful hearing. He was an exception. A paradox. Reporters still climbed his stairs, paying him the homage due an elder statesman. What did his pictures have to tell today's Americans, they wondered? And how were they related to a quiet, meditative life of unvarying routine: winters in Washington Square, summers on Cape Cod, occasional trips in an old green car?

Some of Hopper's rare published statements on the nature of his craft suggest a linkage between subject matter and self. "Great art is the outward expression of an inner life in the artist, and this inner life will result in his personal vision of the world," he wrote in 1953. "The inner life of a human being is a vast and varied realm and does not concern itself alone with stimulating arrangements of color, form, and design."[1] Nonetheless, when *Time* magazine's researchers were at work on a 1956 cover story, a profile of the artist that would confirm his stature as America's premier "Silent Witness," Hopper forbade his sister to say anything to the press about their childhood days in Nyack, New York, or about the family (their father had owned a dry-goods store on South Broadway, Nyack). A year earlier, Hopper had snapped at his wife, Jo, for telling another *Time* staffer that a figure in one of his paintings was looking out the window to check the weather. "Did I say that?" he rumbled. "You're making it Norman Rockwell. From my point of view she's just looking out the window."[2]

Perhaps because he had supported himself until 1924 doing "pot-boiler" illustrations for magazines, Hopper had a horror of anecdote, of narrative. His mature work recoils from any hint of a storyline: the time of day is subject matter enough for any picture. A painting should be as quiet and reticent as the fall of light across a wall. "Maybe I'm not very human," he mused in 1946. "What I wanted to do was to paint sunlight on the side of the house."[3] Besides, narrative involved words and explanations extraneous to the image. Sentiment. Feelings that colored perception and distorted it. "If you could say it in words there'd be no reason to paint," he told a critic determined to wring a drop of human pathos from a vintage Hopper scene of morning light streaming through a shuttered window.[4] "The whole answer is there on the canvas."[5]

In the 1920s and 1930s Hopper had routinely been compared with writers such as Sherwood Anderson and Sinclair Lewis, who satirized the lives lived by the sorts of Americans often found in dingy Main Street storefronts.

Even then, Hopper resented the comparison. But there is a hint of the cigar-smoking George Babbitt, Lewis's famous fictional entrepreneur of the 1920s, in *Sunday* (plate 1), where the foreground is dominated by a figure dressed in the accoutrements of a small-town storekeeper, including pink sleeve garters and a collarless shirt that signals a day of rest. Related by his angular posture to the shapes of the show windows behind him, Hopper's Babbitt, in his very specificity, tilts the meaning of the painting toward a critique, however slight, of the gaudy, go-go, business-driven '20s. As art historian James Thrall Soby observed, Hopper "reveals the sense of desertion and apathy often felt by a people which finds inadequate spiritual absorption in either recreation or work."[6]

The vestige of a story—a Hoboken merchant joylessly faces a Sunday of enforced inertia—harks back to the gritty urban genre associated with the paintings of Robert Henri and his so-called Ash Can School, turn-of-the-century revolutionaries who espoused a new American art based on the life of the streets. After a brief stint at an academy for commercial illustrators, the young Edward Hopper had enrolled at the New York School of Art in 1900, commuting to Manhattan from Nyack and the family store. For the next six years, he studied painting with several of the best-known instructors of the day, including William Merritt Chase and Kenneth Hayes Miller. Robert Henri was the most influential of his teachers, however. Although he would later reject the master's slashing brushwork and dark palette, Hopper derived other lifelong benefits from the Henri class, including an interest in French art of the Impressionist generation, with its emphasis on moments and fragments of time suggested by extreme angles of vision; a friendship with Guy Pène du Bois (his best man and a sympathetic critic); and an abiding admiration for John Sloan, the former newspaper illustrator and Henri associate whose trademark themes and motifs appear with

2. John Sloan. *Picture-Shop Window*. 1907.
Oil on canvas, 32 × 25⅛". The Newark Museum, New Jersey.
Gift of Mrs. Felix Fuld 1925

some regularity in Hopper's paintings of the 1920s.

Picture-Shop Window (fig. 2), for example, is only one of many Sloan canvases to represent the storefront as a key emblem of the urban experience. But while Sloan emphasized the pleasures of consumerism and the delights of seeing people and pictures afresh in the glow of an electrified dusk, Hopper's *Sunday* denies the viewer so much as a glimpse at what the windows may contain. Light can penetrate the storefronts but the human presence is rigorously excluded, just as the lonely figure on the curb has been kept from doing business in his own emporium. If Sloan raised the curtain on the drama of New Yorkers abroad by night, Hopper sent the gesticulating, prattling cast of characters home—except for the bald man sitting still and silent on the curb. He hated illustrating, Hopper said, because the editors wanted noise and bustle, "people waving their arms," too much "posturing and grimacing."[7] Hopper liked Sloan best, he stated in a 1927 appreciation of the latter's work, when the older painter dispensed with the actors and the script and "render[ed] the quality of a brooding and silent interior in this vast city of ours."[8]

John Dos Passos, an old friend who wrote some of his early novels in a Washington Square walkup, remembered coming over to Hopper's studio for tea. The artist often seemed to be on the verge of saying something, Dos Passos thought, "but he never did."[9] Yet the silent Hopper, who eschewed the stories writers live to tell, used imagery in a peculiarly modern way that approximates the new fictional techniques developed by Dos Passos in the early 1930s. In the *U.S.A.* trilogy, for instance, Dos Passos interrupts the narrative with short, stream-of-consciousness sketches called "the Camera Eye" that comment on the content of each book from a different, often oblique, angle by evoking a mood, a sensory impression.[10] This is what Hopper does in *House by the Railroad* (plate 2). The point of view is peculiar: artist and viewer are down below the railroad cut somewhere, unable to find the level ground beneath the house or to gauge how far the colonnaded porch stands from the right-of-way. This is a scene glimpsed casually, as if from a passing car, unresolved, faintly disturbing. This is a mood, an atmosphere of alienation and loss, of heat and sudden coolness in the shadows, without a plot to say whose house this is and where and why it seems so still. Hopper's mansard roof becomes a kind of incipient movie set touched with a whiff of terror that cannot be ascribed wholly to a rational set of clues within the picture—at least until Alfred Hitchcock's *Psycho* fills in the missing storyline in 1960.

The tall mansard also forms an imagistic bridge between Hopper's student days in France and his American maturity. Edward Hopper made three extended trips to Europe between 1906 and 1910. Although he visited Spain and several other countries, Paris was his chief inspiration: he never met Gertrude Stein or Picasso and he remained untouched by the latest "isms" of the avant-garde, but he did study the light and architecture of the city like a belated Impressionist. It was these Paris canvases that Hopper trotted out again and again when asked to show his work in the 1910s and early 1920s—pictures of quais and boulevards defined by buildings crowned with the distinctive flourish of a mansard roof. In his personal iconography, mansards stand for France and culture, and there was irony afoot when Hopper sought out once-elegant mansards in America, a country where progress and fashion deny permanence to any structure, however lovely. In a 1928 essay on Charles Burchfield, a fellow painter of American places, Hopper hints at the transience of America's buildings-up and tearings-down and the tawdry mélange of styles that results from "our native architecture with its hideous beauty. . .pseudo-Gothic, French mansard, Colonial, mongrel or what not, with eye-searing color or delicate harmonies of faded paint."[11] After France, he confessed, America "seemed awfully crude and raw. . .when I got back."[12]

The world looked different to Edward Hopper after Paris. *Corner Saloon* (plate 3) smacks of New York Frenchified, with an elegant gilt scroll of signboard unfurled above a working-class bar. But it is also the Ash Can School's New York—a place once saved from squalor by the energy and dignity of its denizens—with the East Siders John Sloan painted with such life and gusto reduced to faceless blobs of paint. Hopper's people are clearly there on suffrance: the real drama is architectural. Along with the insistent trolley tracks and the lamppost in the foreground, the buildings set the tone for the picture, with the warm red brick of the façade above the bar pitted against the cold blue of smokestacks, gas tanks, factories; if architecture stands for culture, Hopper's America is "crude and raw" indeed.

What did it mean to be an American, then—an American painter, an artist in an artless land? Hopper wrestled with that issue between his final trip to France and his first major exhibition, a show of watercolors at the Frank Rehn Gallery in New York City in 1924 that enabled him to quit commercial art for good. Those years were marked by obscurity and uncertainty, so much so that Alfred Barr, in the catalogue of the 1933 retrospective at The Museum of Modern Art that made Edward Hooper an important American painter almost overnight, created a myth about his lost years. "After a mediocre summer's work in 1915," Barr maintained, "Hopper had virtually given up painting in frustration."[13] But it wasn't that simple. Hopper sold a conventional seascape in 1913 at the Armory Show (ironically, this was the exhibition that introduced modernism to the United States and thus doomed anything so ordinary as seascapes!). Thereafter, his career did founder; he would not sell another work until The Brooklyn Museum bought a watercolor in 1923. Other realist painters turned to abstraction in the wake of the Armory Show; even Henri, that most spontaneous of painters, took to making arcane diagrams of planned compositions. But Edward Hopper instead experimented with new media and new venues. He began to summer regularly along the New England shoreline, in Maine and Massachusetts. And he took up watercolor. *Light at Two Lights* (plate 4), painted at the coast guard station on Cape Elizabeth, just south of Portland, takes a fresh look at two characteristic forms of American vernacular building: the gingerbread house and the beacon—fancy domesticity and stripped-down, nineteenth-century technology—both reduced to primal shapes against the coastal sky. [14] Watercolor does not reward tinkering: the medium helped Hopper seize the pictorial essentials and edit out extraneous distractions. It reinforced his interest in the geometry of architecture, in the dramatic potential of simple masses juxtaposed.

In 1915, with some help from an Australian printmaker,

Hopper learned etching. A complex process, in which success is often judged on the basis of technical mastery of line or tricks of printing, etching served Hopper in a different way. Improvising, working from memory in the studio without models or motifs in front of him, helped the artist to clarify his pictorial vision. The incidentals were pared away. What remained was pure Edward Hopper. "After I took up etchings," he admitted, "my paintings

3. *Evening Wind*. 1921.
Etching, 13¼ × 16". Collection of The Whitney Museum of American Art, New York. Josephine N. Hopper Bequest. 70.1022

seemed to crystallize."[15] The two principal themes that would come to dominate Hopper's painterly iconography—the anonymous, isolated individual and the isolated building that often seems to describe a state of alienation or malaise in the culture as a whole—both appear first in prints.

Evening Wind (fig. 3) is a secular Annunciation scene, the myth of Danae and the shower of gold translated to a frowsy New York flat in which the yearnings of the generic nude rising from her rumpled bed are answered only by the night breeze that stirs the curtains and leaves her all alone. *American Landscape* (fig. 1) marks the beginning, perhaps, of the slow distillation of an idea that would lead to *House by the Railroad* (plate 2). The house that once dominated this rural landscape now shrinks away behind a manmade ridge across the foreground. The railroad track has cut the farmyard off from the pasture, forcing the cows to lumber over the rise as they head for the milking barn. Modernity threatens the natural order: it breeds the sullen isolation spoken of in muttered tones by the placement of the house. "The etching called *American Landscape* has the tang of life as it is lived here and now," Virgil Barker wrote in 1924. "That sharp-edged house could exist nowhere else than in America, and no less characteristic is the long scar of the railroad bed; the. . .clumsy heave of the cows going homeward [is] part of nature's recurrent permanence."[16]

By 1924, the year of his marriage to Jo Nivison, the permanent elements of Hopper's art were all in place: the melancholy, the spareness, the silence, the lonely people, the absence of real narrative, the sense of time passing, the compositions so incisive in their geometry that the real things depicted almost verge on the abstract. The pattern of the Hoppers' life fell into place quickly, too: twin studios high above Washington Square, time on Cape Cod, auto

4. Edouard Manet. *A Bar at the Folies-Bergère*. 1882.
Oil on canvas, 37½ × 51". Courtauld Institute Galleries, London

trips out West, meals in diners, clothes from Sears, movies and the odd play for entertainment. Frugality and concentration. Hopper painted, at most, two or three canvases a year. Jo was always his model, when he needed one. So it is Jo Hopper who stares blankly out from under the brim of a flapper's cloche hat in *Chop Suey (*plate 5), one of a series of restaurant pictures painted in the 1920s showing modest places of the sort the Hoppers frequented.

Like the motel rooms and lobbies Edward Hopper also examined, the restaurant is a public space in which fragments of private life are lived out by common agreement. In restaurants, the most intimate of transactions—dining, with all its sensual associations; conversation; the sharing of hospitality—are conducted under the scrutiny of others (including the viewer and the painter) on a cash basis. The effect, in Hopper's work, is soul-destroying. A wedge of tabletop drives itself between the women taking tea, as if to underscore the fact that nothing passes between them—no word, no touch, no glance. Edouard Manet, a French artist Hopper much admired, caught the same mood in his *A Bar at the Folies-Bergère* (fig. 4). Manet's bored barmaid stares out of the picture at nothing, avoiding the eyes of the customer visible in the mirror behind her, a study in disengagement. So, too, Hopper's flapper seeks the privacy of withdrawal in the bustle of a public place: the light that falls across her powder and mascara, disclosing the face one wears in restaurants and lobbies, acts like the puff of air that wafts through *Evening Wind*, bearing the whisper of concealed, repressed emotion.

The restaurant pictures allude in varying degrees to Manet and to the question of appetite. In *Automat* (plate 6), a plate-glass window replaces Manet's mirror but, instead of human warmth and action, it reflects a chilly, empty space, measured out by a row of identical light fixtures—a sterile machine for eating that kills the appetite and leaves Jo Hopper quite alone, toying with a cup of coffee in the desolate hours of the night. Manet's compote of fruit rests improbably on the windowsill behind her, the luscious forms of the comestibles echoing the shapes of her plump legs and her hat. Like wax fruit, however, Jo is meant to be seen and never tasted. The erotic potential of a midnight encounter is quashed by the cold blue table and the hard blue shadows that guard the figure staring sightlessly into her cup.

For *New York Movie* (plate 7), Jo posed as the young

usherette, leaning against the wall in the hallway of their flat. And she is the "star" of a painting in which the movie and its sparse audience are subordinated to her thoughts: indifferent to the picture show flickering before the eyes of the paying customers, the uniformed girl daydreams a fantasy of her own that lights up the alcove in which she stands and isolates her from the scene. Cut in half by the black rectangle of a wall, that scene—the darkened movie palace, the usherette alone in her pool of light—is as dramatic as any Hollywood encounter. The actors are Jo, his perennial starlet, and Edward Hopper himself, whose preferred point of view, as he stands silently in the back of the theater, watching the usherette, sets the mood for a play that changed little from performance to performance over more than forty years.

In the ledger book recording every major picture he painted, the Hoppers gave the players names and made up stories about how they came to be in movie houses or automats, indulging in the narrative bent the works themselves so often frustrate. Like a B-movie based on a hard-boiled thriller, *Office at Night* (plate 11) is nicknamed "'Confidentially Yours,' Room 2005" in the ledger; the heroine is dubbed "Shirley," and her costume carefully prescribed: "Blue dress, white collar, flesh stockings, black pumps and black hair and plenty of lipstick."[17] But the end result is like a movie still extracted from the flow of the story, or a momentary, voyeuristic peep through a window into a lighted room. What is seen is not at issue—the man, the girl, a battered Underwood, a filing cabinet. Those visual facts have no context, however, despite the erotic charge of the composition in which a faint breeze rustles the window shade, a square of light conjoins the after-hours couple, and Shirley/Jo seems transfixed by a piece of paper that has fallen to the carpet perilously close to the boss's desk. "Any more than this, the picture will have to tell," said Hopper of the ledger entry, "but I hope it will not tell any obvious anecdote, for none is intended."[18]

Hopper once praised "The Killers," an Ernest Hemingway short story set in a diner, for its spare economy of means. "It is refreshing to come upon such honest work . . . after wading through a vast sea of sugar-coated mush that makes up most of our fiction," he declared.[19] In the best of Hopper's work there is the same laconic precision he admired in Hemingway—and some of the sense of barely suppressed, irrational, urban menace that Hollywood got from "The Killers" and from the crime fiction of James M. Cain. *Office at Night* is more terrifying than sexual, or manages to combine the two moods in the deeply troubling way sometimes associated with the film noir style of the 1940s and 1950s.[20] The corrosive tension of *Nighthawks* (plate 10) is heightened by the fact that the hard-faced couple seated side by side at the counter, paired off by posture and twin coffee mugs, never quite touch hands.

There is something suspect, too, something faintly wrong about the commercial places where Hopper's characters fail to make contact. When the actors leave, the sets reveal a treachery of their own. In *Drugstore* (plate 8), the display of purgatives has purged the sidewalk of all life: the storefront blares its huckster's message to an empty street. Hubris. Futility. And emptiness. But what's that? That flash of white, leering around the corner? It stops the heart, at this hour, in this spot, electric with the danger of night in the city, until we recognize . . . a weight machine! The angels carved above the doors of medieval cathedrals used scales to separate the righteous from the wicked. The distinction is harder to make in Hopper's earthbound world of storefronts. In *Seven A.M.* (plate 9) the clock still runs, but the window, with its flyspecked bottles, asks the question posed by all useful things suddenly deprived of function by time or fate: what is a business with no customers, a store with nothing to sell, a consumer culture with nothing left to offer?

Hopper denied putting the "Sunday" in the title of the painting now known as *Early Sunday Morning* (plate 13) because, he said, the word explained too much.[21] It took away the mystery; it limited the mood of emptiness to just one day or time and made the pathos of American storefront enterprise a momentary consequence of blue laws. It made the painting into a Depression-era documentary, like one of Walker Evans's photographs in which the whole, sorry history of a town on the skids could be reconstructed from the texts of the homemade signs propped in the store windows. Hopper took the talkative details out of *Early Sunday Morning*, one by one. The signs say nothing. He painted over a figure that once rested its elbows on the sill of the fourth window from the left, up above the storefronts.[22] He left the image to stand on its own terms, stretching away to red-brick infinity on either side, sad and shabby—and strange, despite its utter ordinariness. Long shadows (cast by what?) ooze down the pavement. A dark form looms up suddenly over the corner of the picture and blots out the sky. And there is no consistent vantage point: some architectural details are viewed from below, or from an oblique angle; others from above, from head on. Furtively, painter and onlooker steal down the empty street, darting glances here and there, pausing only to wonder at the force of light that can tilt a barber pole and cast a shadow longer than life itself.

The oldest, the weightiest of Hopper's commercial blocks exudes an air of transience, of endless movement—an American sensibility, bred of frontiers and highways and yesterdays traded in on narrow hopes for tomorrow. "To me," said Hopper in 1948, "the most important thing is the sense of going on. You know how beautiful things are while you're traveling."[23] *Gas* (plate 12) is a view through a windshield. Perspective drags the eye past the pumps and the attendant, past the lighted windows, toward the place where the highway swoops around a curve and vanishes into the future at the darkest spot in the forest. In *Western Motel* (plate 14), the voyage of life peters out beside a picture window that frames a generic slice of the tourist frontier. Eros and Thanatos: sandwiched between the bed and the hood of the car, Jo poses for one last snapshot before picking up her suitcase, collecting her tall, stooped husband and his coat, and heading off down the highway that curves toward nightfall. Time soon will stop forever. The bedside clock has no hands. The shadows creep across the floor and claim the corner, then the wall.

Toward the end of his life, Hopper worried about how his work would ultimately be regarded. In the 1920s he had seen himself as part of the new American Wave of artists firmly grounded in the observation and straightforward depiction of national life; like Burchfield, he searched out distinctive aspects of the native scene for his subject matter. The critics of the day recognized a fundamental Americanism in Hopper's bare-bones style as well. On the basis of his formal austerity, Guy Pène du Bois called him a Puritan who "will make many of the 'great' moderns seem like reciters of fairy tales."[24] But the danger was that Hopper's perceived Americanism would land him in the camp of the Regionalists, a group of Midwestern painters of American myth and symbol often accused of currying popular favor with the kind of cock-a-doodle-doo narrative the artist professed to loathe.[25] After World War II, with flag-waving Regionalism discredited and Abstract Expressionism in the ascendancy, it became even more urgent to put some distance between himself and the likes of Thomas Hart Benton. Hopper resented attempts to turn him into just another cracker-barrel patriot. "The thing that makes me so mad is the 'American Scene' business," he fumed. "I never tried to do the American scene as Benton and [John Steuart] Curry. . .did. I think [they] caricatured America. I always wanted to do myself."[26]

Although doing one's self sounded like a proposition an action painter might endorse, Hopper was equally chary of abstraction, chastising a friend for comparing the structure of one of his compositions to that of a Mondrian.[27] And efforts to make him into the grandfather of Pop Art were unconvincing.[28] A massive retrospective mounted by The Whitney Museum of American Art in 1964, three years before his death, found Hopper as worried as ever about what the critics might say, while the critics were still unable to slot him into a comfortable pigeonhole somewhere between contemporary abstraction and the obdurate charms of Colonial portraiture. Hopper was—and he remains—an American original. In one sense, his closest affinities of style and content are with the movies, making his painting especially accessible to the new art history of the 1990s, which can acknowledge and applaud the popular component of a work of fine art on its own terms. But Hollywood neither defines nor exhausts the unglittery, unglamorous mystery of Edward Hopper: the fragments of lives, awash in thwarted desire and missed opportunities; the lonely places, out there on the far edge of reality; the dark undercurrent of skepticism about the American Dream; the hideous beauty of commercial America.

NOTES

(For short citations see Further Reading)

1. [Edward Hopper], "Statement by Four Artists," *Reality* 1 (Spring 1953), p. 8.
2. Hopper, quoted in "Gold for Gold," *Time* 65 (May 30, 1955), p. 72. For the 1956 letter to his sister, see Levin, *Edward Hopper*, p.7.
3. Original notation in the Lloyd Goodrich papers, dated April 20, 1946, quoted in Matthew Baigell, "The Silent Witness of Edward Hopper," *Arts* 49 (September 1974), p. 33.
4. Hopper, quoted in "The Silent Witness," *Time* 68 (December 24, 1956), p. 40.
5. Hopper, quoted in Kuh, *The Artist's Voice*, p. 142.
6. Soby, *Contemporary Painters* (New York: The Museum of Modern Art, 1948), p. 37.
7. Hopper, quoted in Archer Winsten, "Washington Square North Boasts Strangers Worth Talking To," *New York Post* (November 26, 1935), and Alexander Eliot, *Three Hundred Years of American Painting* (New York: Time, Inc., 1957), p. 297.
8. Hopper, "John Sloan and the Philadelphians," *The Arts* 11 (April 1927), p. 174.
9. John Dos Passos, quoted in "The Silent Witness," p. 40.
10. See Dos Passos, *1919* (New York: Washington Square Press, 1961), pp. 77–78.
11. Hopper, "Charles Burchfield: American," *The Arts* 14 (July 1928), p. 7.
12. Hopper, quoted in Brian O'Doherty, "Portrait: Edward Hopper," *Art in America* 52 (December 1964), p. 73.
13. Alfred H. Barr, Jr., *Edward Hopper: Retrospective Exhibition* (New York: The Museum of Modern Art, 1933), p. 11.
14. Hobbs, *Edward Hopper*, pp. 84–85.
15. Hopper, quoted in Suzanne Burrey, "Edward Hopper: The Emptying Spaces," *Arts Digest* (April 1, 1955), p. 10.
16. Barker, 'The Etchings of Edward Hopper," *The Arts* 5 (June 1924), p. 325.
17. Ledger entry, quoted in Levin, *Edward Hopper: The Art and the Artist*, p. 58.
18. Hopper, quoted in Levin, *Edward Hopper: The Art and the Artist*, p. 58.
19. Hopper letter of 1927, quoted in Karal Ann Marling, "*Early Sunday Morning*," *Smithsonian Studies in American Art* 2 (Fall 1988), p. 38.
20. See Erika L. Doss, "*Nighthawks* and *Film Noir*," *Postscript: Essays in Film and the Humanities* 2 (Winter 1983), p. 22.
21. Hopper, quoted in Kuh, *The Artist's Voice*, p. 131.
22. See Ernest Brace, "Edward Hopper," *Magazine of Art* 30 (May 1937), p. 275 and Hopper, quoted in O'Doherty, "Portrait," p. 78.
23. Hopper, quoted in "Traveling Man," *Time* 60 (January 19, 1948), p. 60.
24. Guy Pène du Bois, *Edward Hopper* (New York: American Artists Series, 1931), p. 12.
25. ——."The American Paintings of Edward Hopper," *Creative Art* 8 (March 1931), p. 187.
26. Hopper, quoted in O'Doherty, *American Masters*, p. 12.
27. Goodrich, *Edward Hopper*, p. 133.
28. See, for example, São *Paulo 9, Edward Hopper, Environment U.S.A: 1957–1967* (Washington: Smithsonian Institution Press, 1967).

FURTHER READING

Goodrich, Lloyd. *Edward Hopper*. New York: Abrams, 1983.

Hobbs, Robert. *Edward Hopper*. New York: Abrams in association with The National Museum of American Art, 1987.

Kuh, Katherine. *The Artist's Voice: Talks with Seventeen Artists*. New York: Harper and Row, 1962.

Levin, Gail. *Edward Hopper: The Complete Prints*. New York: Norton in association with The Whitney Museum of American Art, 1979.

——. *Edward Hopper: The Art and the Artist*. New York: Norton in association with The Whitney Museum of American Art, 1980.

——. *Edward Hopper*. New York: Crown, 1984.

O'Doherty, Brian. *American Masters: The Voice and the Myth in Modern Art*. New York: Dutton, 1982.

First published in 1992 in the United States of America by Rizzoli International Publications, Inc.
300 Park Avenue South
New York, New York 10010

Copyright ©1992 by Rizzoli International Publications, Inc.
Text copyright ©1992 Karal Ann Marling

Library of Congress Cataloging-in-Publication Data

Marling, Karal Ann.
    Edward Hopper / Karal Ann Marling.
      p.   cm. — (Rizzoli art series)
    Includes bibliographical references.
    ISBN 0-8478-1514-5
    1. Hopper, Edward, 1882–1967. 2. Painters—United States —Biography.   I. Title.   II. Series.
ND237.H75M36   1992
759.13—dc20   91-33473
                                                          CIP

Series Editor: Norma Broude

Series designed by José Conde and Nicole Leong/Rizzoli

Printed in Singapore

Front cover: See colorplate 5

Index to Colorplates

1. *Sunday*. 1926.
Sometimes called *Sunday Hoboken*, this early study of a dejected storekeeper verges on the anecdotal. Hopper would later try to strip away the specifics of storytelling from his work.

2. *House by the Railroad*. 1925.
Hopper suggests the baleful effects of time and modern progress by placing the railroad tracks in the foreground of the painting, while thrusting the principal motif into the background.

3. *Corner Saloon*. 1913.
The quiet drama of the scene arises from the contrast between the warm brick wall of the saloon and the cold tones of the industrial complex at the left.

4. *Light at Two Lights*. 1927.
An emblematic study of technology versus the forces of nature: the isolated lighthouse alludes to the peculiarly modern sense of loneliness that pervades much of Hopper's work.

5. *Chop Suey*. 1929.
Before he gave up commercial illustration, Hopper had created covers for a magazine called *Hotel Management*, which dealt with the ins and outs of the restaurant business.

6. *Automat*. 1927.
Hopper's diners never eat. They linger over cups of cold coffee or tea, lost in their own thoughts. In his mature paintings of eateries, he explored the larger issues of human appetites and basic human contact.

7. *New York Movie*. 1939.
The usherette's daydreams are more appealing than the movie playing in the darkened theater. Hopper's best paintings are like still pictures taken from movies—full of drama but mysterious and strange, without the plot and dialogue.

8. *Drugstore*. 1927.
An empty street, the pathos of a message that nobody gets—even if it is just an advertising display in a store window!

9. *Seven A.M.* 1948.
A mature reprise of *Sunday* (plate 1), this painting also asks what happens to things meant to serve a useful end when they cannot. What is a store without customers? A store where only the clock still works efficiently, to mark the empty hours as the sun creeps into the window and fades the placards?

10. *Nighthawks*. 1942.
Gangsters (and a gun-moll) strayed from a B-movie thriller? Hopper's cast of nocturnal desperadoes gravitates to the light. In "The Killers," a story admired by Hopper, Ernest Hemingway heightened the danger of such places.

11. *Office at Night*. 1940.
The Hoppers called the voluptuous woman in the blue dress "Shirley." Will she bend over to pick up the sheet of paper on the floor? Will the boss look up from his work and meet her glance? The atmosphere is electric with tension. Time stands still.

12. *Gas*. 1940.
A master of misdirection, Hopper uses perspective to plunge the eye toward the spot where the highway vanishes into the darkness, deemphasizing the gas station that seemed to be his subject. The painting is hard to forget, but it is difficult to remember that it includes a human figure. He is there to tend the gas pumps and that is all, a servant of commerce and technology.

13. *Early Sunday Morning*. 1930.
The same commercial block that lurks in the background of *Nighthawks* (plate 9) and other Hopper works becomes the subject. He painted out a figure in an upstairs window to concentrate attention on the place and its inertia. Menacing shadows slip along the pavement. An ominous form—a skyscraper? progress?—blots out the sky at the right.

14. *Western Motel*. 1957.
The painter and the voyeuristic viewer become actors in this bleak little tourist drama. She poses for a snapshot in a room littered with clues that point to an unseen second occupant (a coat, an extra suitcase, a double bed) with a camera—or a paintbrush. Why are we there, too, in their bedroom? And why do we feel so alone?

1. *Sunday*. 1926. Oil on canvas, 29 x 34".
©The Phillips Collection, Washington, D.C.

2. *Hopewell the Railroad*, 1995, Oil on canvas, 24 x 30"

3. *Corner Saloon*. 1913. Oil on canvas, 24 x 29".
Collection of The Museum of Modern Art, New York. Abby Aldrich Rockefeller Fund

4. *Light at Two Lights*. 1927. Watercolor on paper, 13 15/16 x 19 15/16".

5. *Chop Suey*. 1929. Oil on canvas, 32 ⅛ x 38 ⅛".
From the private collection of Barney A. Ebsworth

6. *Automat*. 1927. Oil on canvas, 28 ⅛ x 36".

7. *New York Movie.* 1939. Oil on canvas. 32 ¼ x 40 ⅛".
Collection of The Museum of Modern Art, New York. Given anonymously

8. *Drugstore*, 1927. Oil on canvas, 29 x 40"

9. *Seven a.m.* 1948. Oil on canvas, 30 x 40".
Collection of The Whitney Museum of American Art. Purchase and exchange

10. *Nighthawks*. 1942. Oil on canvas, 33 $\frac{1}{8}$ x 60".
The Art Institute of Chicago. Friends of American Art Collection, 1942.51.

11. *Office at Night*, 1940. Oil on canvas, 22 ½ x 25"

12. *Gas.* 1940. Oil on canvas, 26 ¼ x 40¼".
Collection of The Museum of Modern Art, New York. Mrs. Simon Guggenheim Fund